Sally Social Worker©

You Know You're a Social Worker If …

written by
Laura Frohboese, MSW, LCSW

illustrated by
Greg Russell

D1411078

Dedicated to all of the other Sally Social Workers out there working hard for the fortune, glamour and prestige

Special thank you to Mom, Dad, Pam and Rich for all of your support, encouragement, collaboration, empowerment and other great social work buzz words

YOU KNOW YOU'RE A SOCIAL WORKER IF ...

You think $40,000 a year is "really making it."

You don't really know what it's like to work with men, wear a suit to work, or go on business trips.

YOU KNOW YOU'RE A SOCIAL WORKER IF ...

You know the numbers for the suicide hotline, shelters, food pantries, detoxes and social services right off the top of your head, but you have to look up your friends' numbers.

YOU KNOW YOU'RE A SOCIAL WORKER IF ...

You tell people what you do, and they say...

You've had two or more jobs at one time just to pay the bills.

You have had to explain to people that not all social workers take away kids.

You spend more than half your day documenting and doing paperwork.

YOU KNOW YOU'RE A SOCIAL WORKER IF ...

You think nothing of discussing child abuse over dinner with your social worker friends.

You can make just about anything a strength.

YOU KNOW YOU'RE A SOCIAL WORKER IF ...

You know a lot of other social workers who have left the profession to do something else. Staying at a job for two years is a "long time."

YOU KNOW YOU'RE A SOCIAL WORKER IF ...

You work odd hours and wonder why others can't also be as flexible, or why we have to be the only ones who work strange hours.

Your friends know not to ask how you know people who say hi to you in public.

YOU KNOW YOU'RE A SOCIAL WORKER IF ...

You've learned to get really good at setting limits.

Your professional newsletters always have articles about rising salaries ... but you still haven't seen it.

YOU KNOW YOU'RE A SOCIAL WORKER IF ...

You've gone to several seminars on burnout prevention or "compassion fatigue."

YOU KNOW YOU'RE A SOCIAL WORKER IF ...

You can't imagine working at a bank or crunching numbers all day.

$1 + 1 = 2$

$13 + 24 = 37$

$36 \times 57 = 2,052$

$62,895 \div 365 = 172.72$

SallySocialWorker.com

YOU KNOW YOU'RE A SOCIAL WORKER IF ...

You've had clients who liked you just a little *too* much.

Having lunch is a luxury many days.

YOU KNOW YOU'RE A SOCIAL WORKER IF ...

You've been cursed at or threatened … and it doesn't bother you.

Your job orientation has included personal safety classes.

You have the best stories … but you can't share any of them.

You cringe when people outside the field talk about how "crazy" their days are because they have meetings and conference calls.

Your parents don't know half the stuff that you've dealt with at your job.

You are considered an "expert" on financial assistance for your low-income individuals, but you can't keep your own checkbook balanced.

Despite all the stress, you truly love what you do and couldn't imagine doing anything else.

ABOUT THE AUTHOR

Laura Frohboese earned her MSW from Boston College in 1997 and has worked in community-based settings, social service agencies, medical and psychiatric hospitals, clinics and private practice settings. She currently has a small private counseling practice and works in an ER in Charlotte, NC. Laura combines her passion for social work, corny sense of humor and love of public speaking by giving talks about the value of humor in clinical practice and preventing compassion fatigue.

ABOUT THE ILLUSTRATOR

Greg Russell studied Communication Arts at East Carolina University. When he graduated, he hit all of the ad agencies looking for a job. "Well, Gregory," each one would ask, "what do you do? Graphics or illustration?" He told them, "I do both!" They replied, "Come back when you decide which you want to do." After 30 years, Greg is still doing both graphics and illustration. He designs and produces books, designs ads, draws cartoons and caricatures, paints, sculpts, does photography and builds websites. Some people never get anything right. His work can be found at Facebook.com/GregRussellGraphics.

Made in the USA
Lexington, KY
30 April 2018